Marcella Umbrella
and the "What Ifs"

Jess Mey

Marcella Umbrella sat awake in her bed. She groaned, "How can I sleep with so much stuff in my head?"

1

She tossed and she turned
and she laid upside down,
but just couldn't stop her thoughts
from running around.

2

She heard a loud creak come from her big bedroom door, and saw Mom's tall shadow spread across the wood floor.

3

What if I forgot to put toys away,

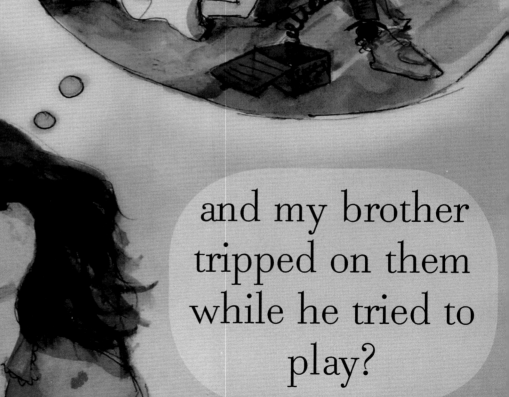

and my brother tripped on them while he tried to play?

6

Marcella just cried
as she thought of the stuff

that made her
quite sad til
she'd had quite
enough.

9

"How can I not feel so scared?" she asked Mom.

And Mom sat on the bed, smiled, and looked very calm.

10

Have you seen the bad guys from the books that you've read?

13

Or stepped into quicksand and sunk into the ground?

15

When everything's scary,
you must try to laugh.

You might still be frightened,
but you'll cut it in half.

But, "What if,"
Marcella started to say,

and Mom said,
"We can't make all
bad go away."

"But we CAN choose to focus
on all that is good,
and not focus on 'what if,'
'should,' 'could,' or 'would.'

18

And it's important
that you also talk
about fears,

to your teacher, your doctor,
or me. I'm all ears."

19

"Remember to not believe all that you think, and slowly those fears will begin to shrink."

Marcella sat quietly, staring at Mom, then said, "I'm still nervous, but it's ALMOST all gone."

Mom hugged Marcella and patted her head, then stood up and tucked Marcella in bed.

23

About Jessica

Jessica Mey was inspired to write Marcella's story based on her experience with anxiety that started at age five. She says that *Marcella Umbrella and the "What Ifs"* is the book she wished she had as a child. Jessica lives just outside of Pittsburgh, PA with her husband, Mike, and their corgi, Bowie.

Made in the USA
Middletown, DE
19 March 2018